Getting To Know...

Nature's Children

CROCODILES

Peter Carver

SCHOLASTIC INC.

New York   Toronto   London   Auckland   Sydney
Mexico City   New Delhi   Hong Kong   Buenos Aires

Facts in Brief

Classification of Crocodiles

      Class: *Reptilia* (reptiles)
      Order: *Crocodilia* (crocodilians)
      Family: *Crocodylidae* (crocodile family)
      Genus: There are 3 genera of crocodiles.
      Species: There are over 14 species of crocodiles.

World distribution. Tropical regions in southern North America, Central and South America, Asia, Africa, Madagascar, Australia and islands in the western Pacific Ocean.

Habitat. Rivers, lakes, swamps and wetlands, and open saltwater.

Distinctive physical characteristics. Dark green, gray or black skin; short legs with webbed feet and large powerful tail; ears and nostrils located on upper surface of long narrow head; even when closed, jaws show almost all teeth.

Habits. Solitary or, during feeding and breeding, in groups dominated by large male. Basks on sandy or muddy banks near water's edge. Female buries eggs in sand or builds nest of leaves and mud.

Diet. Fish, birds and mammals.

Published by Scholastic Inc.
90 Old Sherman Turnpike, Danbury, Connecticut 06816.

SCHOLASTIC and associated logos are trademarks of Scholastic Inc.

ISBN 0-7172-6692-3   Printed in the U.S.A.

Have you ever wondered . . .

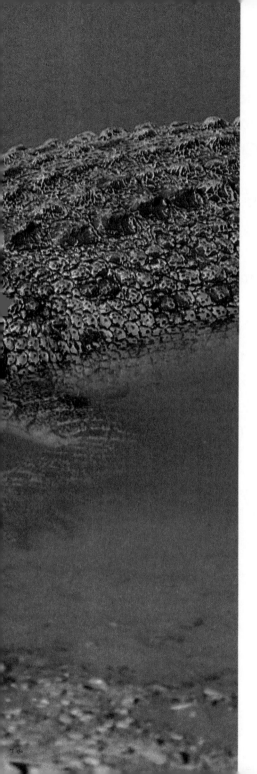

Long ago in Egypt the crocodile was considered holy. Temples were built in honor of gods pictured with crocodile heads, and the people even named one of their cities Crocodilopolos. Sacred crocodiles were kept in captivity, bedecked with gold bracelets and fed special food. When they died they were embalmed and wrapped in cloth as mummies, just like the great pharaohs, or kings, who were buried in the Pyramids.

Although crocodiles are no longer treated this way, people still find them both fascinating and terrifying. And they still cling to many mistaken notions about their habits and behavior. Let's try to find out what these mysterious and misunderstood creatures are really like.

Ancient Crocodiles

Crocodilian is the name given to a group of reptiles that includes crocodiles, alligators, gavials and caimans. Crocodilians have been around for a long time. They first appeared on the Earth more than 200 million years ago during a time known as the Age of Dinosaurs or the Age of Reptiles. The largest grew to be 15 metres (50 feet) long and probably snacked on dinosaurs.

Although dinosaurs eventually died out as climates changed and entire continents shifted, crocodilians survived. One reason may have been that they were able to hunt both on land and in the water. This gave them more flexibility when food became scarce. Surprisingly the crocodilians that exist today are very similar to their ancient ancestors.

*This crocodile is known as the
false gavial because of its long
narrow snout and its diet of fish.*

Reptile Relatives

Crocodiles, alligators, caimans and gavials all have a long snout filled with teeth, short legs, a long tail and thick scaly skin. So how do you tell one crocodilian from another? Mainly by the shape of their snout and where they live.

Gavials, or gharials as scientists prefer to call them, live in large rivers in India. They have 100 small teeth and a very narrow snout, that is the perfect shape for catching fish and frogs. They are one of the largest crocodilians, reaching a length of 7 metres (23 feet). Most caimans are much smaller than gavials and they have a broad snout. They are found in rivers, lakes and swamps from Mexico to Argentina.

Of all the crocodilians, alligators and crocodiles are the ones people tend to hear more about and are most likely to confuse. However, crocodiles are generally more active than alligators, and they have a narrower head and a more pointed snout. If you still aren't sure which is which, take a look at their teeth. Most of a crocodile's teeth are visible even when its mouth is closed. And you might notice that the extra

Alligator

Crocodile

large fourth tooth on either side of its lower jaw fits into a notch on the *outside* of its upper jaw. The alligator also has two enlarged teeth in its lower jaw, but they fit into a special hole *inside* its mouth and can't be seen when its mouth is closed. The ranges of the crocodile and the alligator overlap only in southern Florida.

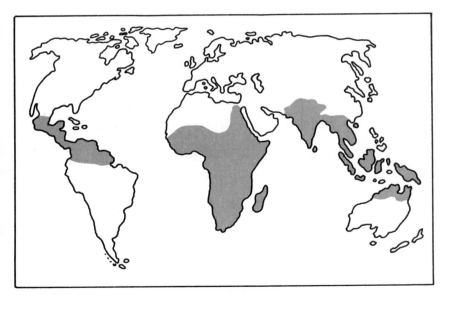

The shaded areas on this map show where crocodiles can be found.

Cold-Blooded Creatures

A crocodile is a reptile—but what's a reptile? Reptiles include animals such as snakes, turtles and lizards. They have a backbone—unlike creatures like worms—and they breathe air. Many spend part of their lives in water, but they must come to the surface to breathe. They also have dry scaly skin.

Another characteristic of reptiles is that they lay eggs from which their young hatch. Female reptiles go onto the land to lay their eggs. Unlike amphibians, whose young have a larval stage, reptile offspring develop directly. In fact, many types look exactly like small versions of their parents when they hatch.

Crocodiles, like other reptiles, are cold-blooded. This doesn't mean that their blood is actually cold but just that the temperature of their blood adjusts to the temperature of their surroundings. Crocodiles live in warm climates, so it is fairly easy for them to keep their bodies at a comfortable temperature level.

Soaking up the sun.

Crocodiles are considered the world's most intelligent reptiles. (Pygmy crocodile)

All Kinds of Crocodiles

There are 14 species of crocodiles living in the world today. Most live near freshwater or brackish swampy waters near sea coasts. They prefer slow-moving shallow water to large lakes or the open sea. Crocodiles are found in tropical regions in southern North America, Central and South America, Asia, Africa, Australia and islands in the western Pacific Ocean.

Crocodiles range in size from 8 metres (26 feet) to dwarf varieties that grow to be just over a metre (not quite 4 feet) long. The Indopacific, or saltwater, crocodile is the largest member of the family and also the largest reptile in the world. It is also the only type that will swim far out to sea—up to 1000 kilometres (600 miles). The smallest crocodiles are the West African and Congo dwarf crocodiles that inhabit tropical forests in Western Africa. The best-known variety is the Nile crocodile. It grows to be over 5 metres (16.5 feet) long and may weigh almost a tonne. It lives in most parts of Africa except in the Sahara and northwest areas.

Champion Swimmers

Opposite page:
You could never win a swimming race with a Johnston's crocodile — it's too fast.

Water is where crocodiles feel most at home. It's where they raise their young, feed and spend long hours quietly floating around.

The crocodile's body is perfectly suited to life in the water. Its short stubby legs aren't used for swimming, but are tucked close to its sides. It moves forward swiftly by swinging its long powerful tail from side to side. Its eyes and nostrils are on top of its head, so it can remain motionless in the water while still being able to see and breathe. When crocodiles dive underwater they close their nostrils and special ear flaps to keep out the water. And they are excellent at holding their breath—they can stay submerged for 30 minutes at a time.

Since crocodiles don't have any lips, water flows into their mouth when they are underwater. However, they don't have to worry about swallowing it because they have a special valve in their throat. This valve can be closed off so that water will not flow into their breathing passages. It also allows them to hold prey in their jaws or even eat underwater.

The Race Is On

Even though crocodiles spend a large part of their lives in water, they have been known to cover quite long distances overland. Nile crocodiles, for instance, have been seen up to 10 kilometres (6 miles) from the nearest river or swamp. Such journeys are made to find food or new bodies of water when their previous swimming hole has dried up. A crocodile on land looks clumsy, but in fact, it moves quite efficiently on its thick strong legs, and its webbed feet keep it from sinking into the mud.

Crocodiles move at four different speeds on land. Most often they can be seen slithering from riverbanks into the water on their bellies when they've been disturbed. However, their squat legs are strong enough to support their entire body and allow them to walk with their belly completely off the ground, although their tail does drag along behind. More surprisingly, a crocodile can run—and run faster than a human being over a short distance. One crocodile— Johnston's crocodile of northern Australia—has actually been known to *gallop*.

Opposite page:
A Nile crocodile venturing out onto land.

Open Wide

How many teeth do you think a crocodile has? If you said between 60 and 80 you're absolutely right. And when one tooth falls out another soon grows in its place.

A crocodile with its mouth wide open is a frightening sight. But you might be amazed to learn that its cone-shaped teeth aren't especially sharp and are of no use for chewing. Thanks to the crocodile's super-strong jaw muscles, however, they make an excellent weapon against intruders and are perfect for catching hold of and tearing prey. If the prey is small enough a crocodile will simply swallow it whole.

If you are close enough to count a crocodile's teeth, you are much too close!

18

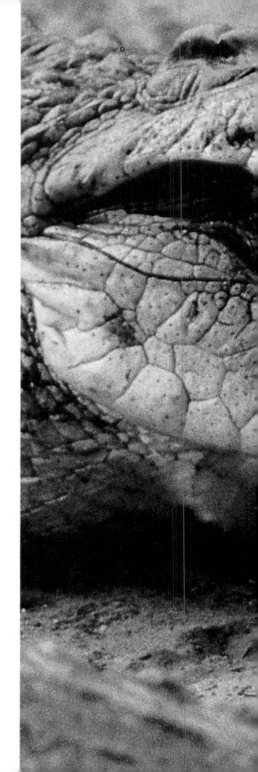

Feeding Time

The crocodile is a skillful hunter. It floats just below the surface of the water with only its nostrils and eyes showing. It can stay so still that it is often mistaken for a log... until a fish, a bird or an animal is within reach. Then, snap! The great jaws open and clamp shut on the unsuspecting prey. It's almost impossible to pry open those jaws if the crocodile wants to keep them shut because of its powerful muscles.

Some crocodiles wait in the water where they know animals will come to drink. Then they grasp the animal by its nose or front legs or use a well-aimed swat of their tail to knock it into the water. Small prey is eaten immediately, while large prey is pulled deep into the water and kept there till it drowns.

What does a crocodile consider a delicious meal? Well, it wouldn't turn up its snout at much. It likes all kinds of fish, birds and mammals. In fact, it will eat just about anything it can catch—if it's hungry that is. Crocodiles don't usually feed every day and they will ignore their usual prey if they have a full stomach.

Opposite page:
Watching . . . and waiting . . .

Lazy Lifestyle

In general, the crocodile has a relaxed lifestyle. Most types hunt during the night. As soon as the sun comes up, they climb out of the water and find a comfortable spot to lie in the sunshine and soak up the rays. You may have seen photos of crocodiles on land with their mouths open. They aren't angry or hungry as you might expect, they are just a little bit too warm. By opening their mouth they are able to release excess moisture and heat, just as a dog does when it pants.

While relaxing in the sun, crocodiles in some areas may be visited by a small bird called an oxpecker. It perches on the back of the large reptile and then proceeds to peck bugs and any other creatures from its skin. While the crocodile sunbathes it gets a good cleaning as well.

A panting Cuban crocodile and a cooler companion.

Special Skin

The skin of the crocodile is designed for its watery lifestyle. Its thick hide helps to keep the water out. The dark brownish black color of the crocodile's skin helps it to absorb as much sunlight and warmth as possible. It also allows the crocodile to blend into the swampy surroundings it generally prefers.

Unfortunately as well as helping the crocodile to survive, its skin has almost brought about its extinction in certain areas. The scaly belly skin is highly valued as leather to make shoes, handbags, wallets and belts. So many crocodiles were killed for their skin that all species were at one time considered endangered. This situation has improved somewhat since crocodiles are now protected in many parts of the world.

A close up of a crocodile's scaly skin.

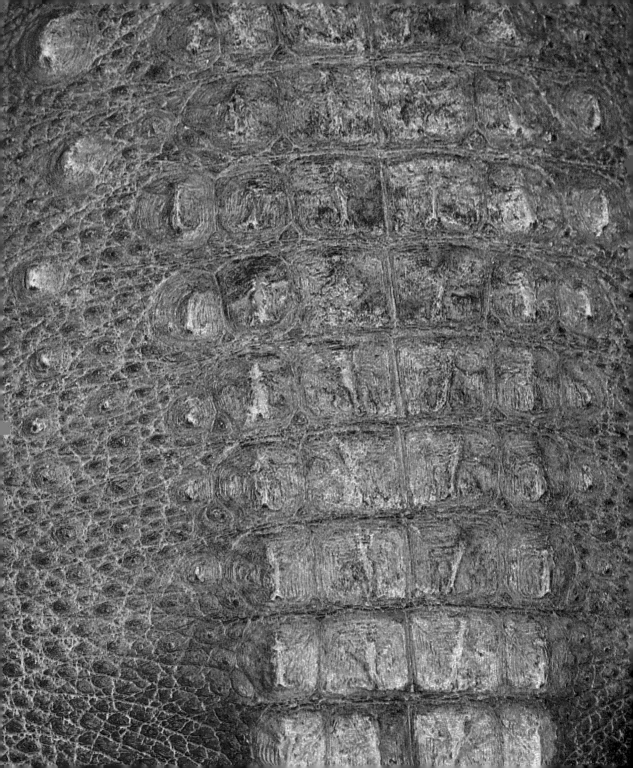

Sights and Sounds

Crocodiles are active at night, and like many other nocturnal animals they have eyes with vertical slit-shaped pupils. These widen in the dark to let in as much light as possible. Inside their eyes is a special reflective material—which your pet cat also has—to make use of all the available light.

Like many other animals that do a lot of diving or spend a lot of time in the water, the crocodile has an extra set of transparent eyelids. By closing them, it can protect its eyes underwater and still see fairly well.

The crocodile has excellent hearing and may rely on it for hunting even more than on its eyesight. Its ears are located on top of its head right behind its eyes. They are able to hear even the smallest sound when the crocodile is lying motionless in the water.

Crocodiles also have a well-developed sense of smell.

Saltwater crocodile.

Let's Talk

You might wonder how crocodiles communicate with one another. They make a number of noises, each of which means something different. An angry crocodile hisses, especially a female guarding her nest. During mating season, romantic couples grunt at each other to show affection. A crocodile defending its territory roars while spraying water in all directions. Neighbors will answer with roars of their own. Young crocodiles chirp or grunt softly at their mother and squeak or squeal when they're in danger. And sometimes crocodiles have been known to bark, although no one is certain just what that means.

Like many animals, crocodiles also communicate with body language. A raised head, a thrashing tail, a long measuring look all send messages that other crocodiles are quick to understand.

It doesn't take a crocodile expert to figure out that this crocodile is warning you to back off.

A pair of young Nile crocodiles cruising.

Keep Out

Crocodiles are solitary reptiles for the most part. Almost all types prefer to live on their own. Each crocodile has a territory that includes both land area and water that it defends from other crocodiles. Female territories, however, may overlap those of the males.

An adult may have the same territory for years unless the water dries up or there isn't enough food. Young crocodiles may have to relocate several times if a larger and older crocodile decides to take over their area.

A loud roar is usually all that is needed to warn an intruder to leave another crocodile's territory. Rarely will a crocodile actually have to defend its area by using its powerful jaws.

Nile crocodiles are unusual because they don't have separate territories except during mating season. They spend much of their time in groups basking on riverbanks together and searching for schools of fish to eat. Johnston's crocodiles may also gather together during the dry season when deep pools may be few and far between.

Getting Together

Somewhere between the ages of five and ten a crocodile mates for the first time. During the mating season large older males stake out an area and allow only females and young males to share it. They defend this territory fiercely from competing males and in the rare cases where a rival persists, fighting may continue until the death of one or the other.

A male shows he is interested in a female by swimming near her and splashing water around with his tail and snout. The couple then circle together, grunting at each other. Mating takes place in the water. They separate soon afterwards and the male does not take part in guarding the eggs or rearing the young.

Crocodile love.

Female African crocodile guarding her nest in a sandy riverbank.

Watchful Mothers

Soon after mating the female crocodile builds a nest near the water. Usually the eggs are laid during the dry season so that the young will hatch during the wet season when food is plentiful. Some crocodiles lay their eggs in leaves to help keep them warm. Others bury them in the sand in a sunny spot. The female lays between 25 and 90 eggs that resemble long chicken eggs with shiny shells. Then she guards the nest, sometimes going without food. Lizards, birds, mongooses and even some crocodiles consider the eggs a tasty treat.

The eggs usually take three months to hatch. Just before hatching the crocodile mother hears squeaking and chirping sounds coming from the inside of the eggs. This is the signal for her to dig up the nest. Then she may carry the eggs to the water in her mouth, or she may wait until they hatch and lead her offspring to the water or carry them a few at a time in her mouth. The hatchlings break out of the egg using a small pointed egg tooth on the top of their snout. The tooth drops off soon after the baby hatches.

Hungry Hatchlings

The hatchlings are usually 15 to 25 centimetres (6 to 10 inches) long and they look like tiny versions of their parents. They are able to swim as soon as they enter the water. The next thing they do is to start eating. Breaking out of an egg is hard work and makes them hungry. The baby crocodiles begin by chasing and eating insects. Unlike most reptile mothers, the female crocodile watches over her young for the first few weeks of their lives, and in some cases for several months. Her offspring stay very close to her at the beginning. In fact, they usually crawl all over her head and body.

This is a dangerous time for young crocodiles because they have so many enemies and so few defenses. Birds, fish and even adult crocodiles may gobble them up. They try to remain hidden as much as possible and rely on their mother for protection.

It's hatching day!

Hitching a ride. (Thailand crocodiles)

Bigger and Bigger

Young crocodiles soon progress from eating bugs to stalking frogs, fish and birds. In no time at all they are competent hunters. And little by little as they grow larger they are able to manage on their own.

For the first few years crocodiles grow about 30 centimetres (a foot) each year. After that they grow more slowly, but some keep growing all their lives. No one is sure exactly how long crocodiles can live. In captivity they have survived for up to 40 years, but scientists believe that a few of the giant ones in the wild may be over 100 years old!

Man-Eaters?

Crocodiles have a reputation for being ferocious man-eaters that will go out of their way to find a human being to devour. This is simply not true. Not too suprisingly, some of the largest varieties have been known to eat a human who happens along when they are hungry, and any crocodile will attack if it is cornered or if someone gets too close to its nesting site.

Most crocodiles, however, prefer to avoid contact with people altogether. Adult crocodiles have no natural predators. The only living thing that threatens them is man.

Extreme caution should always be used when crocodiles are nearby.

Who Would Miss the Crocodile?

It is important for people to realize that crocodiles aren't evil creatures and that they play a significant and useful role in life in tropical regions. Enormous numbers of crocodiles are still being killed for their skin, and swamps are being filled in and changed into farmland, destroying their habitats. The resulting decrease in the crocodile population has already had an impact. For instance, Nile crocodiles eat large fish that prey upon the smaller fish that are an important food source for the people of the area. As the number of crocodiles decreases, the number of large fish increases and there are fewer small fish for people to catch and eat.

Fortunately people are coming to realize the important role crocodiles play in the world. They are protected by law in many countries, and reserves have been set up for them. As well, special farms are hatching crocodile eggs and then later returning the young to the wild. With conservation and better understanding, the outlook for these amazing reptiles is beginning to improve.

Relaxing after a hard day of hunting and sun bathing. (Mugger, or marsh crocodile)

Words to Know

Amphibians   A group of animals that live both on land and in water. Frogs, toads and salamanders are amphibians.

Cold-blooded   Term used for animals that have no automatic internal control of their body temperature.

Egg tooth   A tooth-like point on a crocodile's snout used to help it crack out of its egg.

Hatch   To emerge from an egg.

Hatchling   Newly hatched crocodile.

Mating season   Time during which animals come together to produce young.

Predator   An animal that hunts other animals for food.

Prey   Animal that other animals hunt for food.

Reptile   Class of cold-blooded animals that includes crocodiles, snakes, turtles and lizards.

Territory   Area that an animal or a group of animals lives in and often defends from animals of the same kind.

INDEX

Cover Photo: Australia Info Service
Photo Credits: Breck P. Kent, pages 4, 15, 16, 23, 24, 25, 31, 35, 43; Bill Ivy, pages 7, 12, 27; Four By Five inc., page 11; Robert Winslow, page 19; Christopher R. Harris (Shostal Associates), page 20; Tom McHugh (Photo Researchers, inc.), page 28; Tim Tuten (Black Star), page 32; Tony Dawson, page 36; New York Zoological Society, page 39; Phyllis Greenberg, page 40; G. Ziesler (Peter Arnold, inc.), page 45; Boyd Norton, page 46.

Getting To Know...

Nature's Children

KANGAROOS

Bill Ivy

SCHOLASTIC INC.

New York   Toronto   London   Auckland   Sydney
Mexico City   New Delhi   Hong Kong   Buenos Aires

Facts in Brief

Classification of kangaroos

Class:	*Mammalia* (mammals)
Order:	*Marsupialia* (pouch-bearing mammals)
Family:	*Macropodidae* (kangaroo family)
Subfamilies:	*Macropodinae* (kangaroos)
	Potorinae (rat kangaroos)
Genus:	There are 17 genera of kangaroos.
Species:	There are over 50 species of kangaroos.

World distribution. Kangaroos are found in Australia, New Guinea and on nearby islands.

Habitat. Varies with species.

Distinctive physical characteristics. Most kangaroos have large back paws, small front paws and a large tail. The females have a pouch in which they carry their young.

Habits. Most live in groups, moving about by hopping on their large back paws and feeding from dusk to dawn.

Diet. Most eat mainly grass.

Published by Scholastic Inc.
90 Old Sherman Turnpike, Danbury, Connecticut 06816.

SCHOLASTIC and associated logos are trademarks of Scholastic Inc.

ISBN 0-7172-6692-3

Printed in the U.S.A.

Have you ever wondered . . .

When the English explorer Captain James Cook
was in Australia in 1770, he saw a strange
animal unlike anything he had ever seen before.
It was almost as tall as he was and had a
deer-like head with long ears. The animal had
short forearms and a very long tail and it carried
its young in a pouch on its stomach. Not only
that, it stood upright and hopped around on its
two strong hind legs! Can you guess what
Captain Cook saw? Right—it was a kangaroo!

Today almost everyone is familiar with this
unusual animal. However, there are a lot of
interesting kangaroo facts you might not know.
For example, did you know that some
kangaroos are no larger than a rabbit and that
others live in trees? To learn more about these
fascinating animals, read on. Kangaroos are full
of surprises.

Meet the amazing kangaroo—
Australia's national animal.

Marsupials

Animals whose young are fed and cared for in their mother's pouch are called *marsupials*. Kangaroos are the largest of these pouched animals, but they're not the only ones. Other marsupials include wombats, numbats, bandicoots, koalas, Tasmanian devils and opossums. Except for opossums, which are found in the Americas, all marsupials live in Australia, New Guinea and islands in that area.

These animals have pouches because their young are born premature: their eyes, back legs and tail are not developed yet, and each one is only about the size of a jellybean! Since the baby marsupial is not ready to meet the world, it needs time to feed and grow in a warm, safe environment. Its mother's pouch is the perfect place.

Although rock wallabies usually spend the day in caves, this mother and joey are out basking in the sun.

Living Down Under

Kangaroos live in the wild in Australia, New Guinea and on nearby islands. A few species have been introduced to New Zealand and the red-necked wallaby has been introduced to the United Kingdom. Depending on the type, a kangaroo may live in desert, swamp or forest areas, among rocks or cliffs or high up in trees.

Describing a typical kangaroo is not easy since they come in a variety of sizes, shapes and colors. Let's look at a few of the different types of kangaroo.

*Opposite page:
Rock wallabies
are much smaller
than gray and red
kangaroos.*

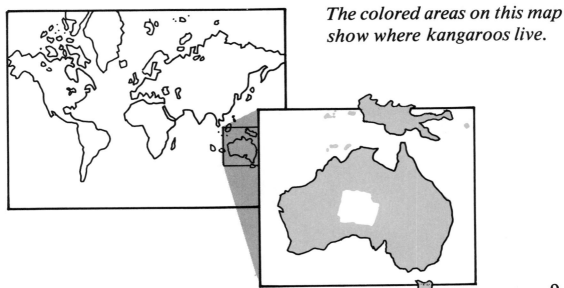

*The colored areas on this map
show where kangaroos live.*

Big Red

Meet "big red," the tallest of the kangaroos. Often standing almost 2 metres (7 feet) tall, red kangaroos can easily look over an average person's head. They weigh up to 90 kilograms (198 pounds). Most male reds have reddish fur similar in color to that of a deer, but the females are usually a blue-gray color. They weigh less than the males and can travel faster. This has earned them the nickname "blue fliers." In some areas, however, the females are red and the males are bluish-gray.

The red kangaroo lives on grasslands and inland plains. During the mating season the male secretes a red substance on his throat and chest. He then rubs this on his back with his forepaws, dyeing the fur an even brighter red. Supposedly this added color impresses the females.

This red kangaroo looks very relaxed, but let there be the least hint of danger and it will be off like a shot.

The Great One

The great gray kangaroo is the heavyweight of its family and the largest of all marsupials. This is the kangaroo you are most likely to see at the zoo. Although it is not always as tall as the red kangaroo, it is usually stronger and heavier.

The Eastern gray kangaroo lives in open forests on the east coast of Australia. Its soft fur ranges in color from mainly gray to brown and its tail has a black tip. The Western gray kangaroo, which is a dark, muddy gray, is found on the west coast. These large kangaroos communicate with a number of sounds including clucks, coughs and loud growls.

Like most of their relatives, gray kangaroos feed mainly on grass.

Middleweights

Most small- to medium-sized members of the kangaroo family are known as wallabies. They have larger feet (in relation to their size), a more hairy tail and smaller front teeth than other kangaroos. They weigh anywhere from 1.8 to 22 kilograms (4 to 50 pounds).

Some wallabies are named for their habitats. Rock wallabies live in caves. Brush wallabies live in areas covered in small trees and shrubs.

Other species are named for one of their physical traits or habits. Hare wallabies are about the same size as hares, behave like them in some ways and can bound with incredible speed. The nail-tailed wallaby has a scale like a small fingernail at the tip of its tail, and the pretty face wallaby . . . well, you get the idea.

This wallaby almost seems to be posing for the photographer.

Walla-Who?

If you take the word wallaby and mix it with the word kangaroo you get "wallaroo." This is the name for a kind of kangaroo that is smaller than the great grays and reds but larger than the wallabies. Wallaroos are often mistaken for their larger relatives, but there are visible differences. Wallaroos are sturdier and have shorter legs. Also called euros or hill kangaroos, they make their home among rocky outcrops and gullies. Their fur is long and coarse and ranges in color from reddish brown to dark blue gray.

Wallaroos can survive on land with little vegetation and very little water as long as there are places such as caves where they can hide from the heat. If they get thirsty they dig in the ground for water with their forepaws. They can dig as deep as one metre (3 feet)!

Some wallaroos have been known to go without water for more than a month.

Above the Rest

You wouldn't think to look for a kangaroo in a tree but that's exactly where tree kangaroos make their home. These kangaroos are built differently than their ground-dwelling cousins. Their front and hind limbs are about the same length and the nails on their front feet are long and curved—ideal for climbing. The soles of their wide, short feet are covered with rough cushion-like pads that prevent them from slipping. Their long tail provides balance for climbing and jumping.

The tree kangaroo is an excellent climber and quite an acrobat. It jumps nimbly from branch to branch and can leap 18 metres (50 feet) to the ground. Once on land it moves along by hopping quickly.

Tree kangaroos live mainly in rain forests. They tend to spend the day in the trees eating leaves and fruit, coming down at night to feed on the herbs that are only available on the ground. But should an enemy appear, they quickly head back to the safety of the tree.

Opposite page:
To reach the ground, tree kangaroos will jump or climb down tail first.

Rat Packs

At first glance it is hard to believe that rat kangaroos are kangaroos at all. In fact, they are so different from the others that they have their own branch on the kangaroo family tree.

There are ten kinds of rat kangaroos and the largest is about the size of a rabbit. They generally live alone in a variety of habitats and feed on roots, insects, fungi and worms. During the day some types sleep in nests of grass which they gather with their tail. One species, the boodie, even sleeps in an underground burrow. The musky rat kangaroo, the smallest of all the kangaroos, has a hairless, scaly tail, five toes on each foot and often walks on all fours.

As its name indicates, the musky rat kangaroo has a strong musky smell.

By Leaps and Bounds

You will never see a kangaroo run. Instead it bounces along on its powerful back legs, using its long tail for balance. While the bigger kangaroos usually travel at about 20 kilometres (12 miles) an hour, they can go well over twice that fast for short distances. When moving at top speed, a red or a great gray can easily leap 8 metres (25 feet) with each hop, as if it had springs in its feet. And one jump can take it as high as a basketball hoop, although most of the time they only jump about half that high.

How does the kangaroo do it? Inside each leg is a tendon, like a large elastic band, which attaches the powerful leg muscle to the bone. When the kangaroo lands its legs bend, stretching this tendon tight and causing the muscle to contract. On its next jump the leg muscle stretches and the tendon snaps back to its original size. This propels the kangaroo forward.

Although kangaroos do a lot of hopping, that's not the only way they get from place to place. Sometimes, including when they graze, they move around slowly on all fours.

Big Foot

Members of the main kangaroo family are known as *macropods*, a word that means big feet. The kangaroo certainly deserves its name. Depending on the species, its feet can be up to 45 centimetres (18 inches) long.

Most kangaroos have only four toes, the big toe having disappeared in all but the musky rat kangaroo. As well, the second and third toes are joined together, forming a "twin toe" that the kangaroo uses to comb its fur. The fourth toe is the largest and provides the most support for the body. It has two nails close together that serve as tweezers for removing pesky ticks.

Compared to its back paws, the kangaroo's front paws are very small and have five fingers. Unlike you, the kangaroo can't bring its thumb around to meet its fingers, so it can't grasp things easily.

Can you guess what kind of wallaby this is? It's a pretty face wallaby.

Life with the Mob

A herd of kangaroos is called a mob. The average mob contains 10 to 20 members. It is usually made up of males, or boomers, females, or does, and young of all ages. Each mob is led by an "old man," the strongest and usually the largest boomer.

A kangaroo mob is a rather loose-knit group. Some members may join the gang for only a few days while others may stay for years. The only real bonds that exist are between a mother and her young.

Mobs are usually on the move searching for food and water. In general, kangaroos prefer to feed from dusk to dawn, but in the cooler winter months they may also feed during the day. Kangaroos are fairly sociable and it is not unusual to see many mobs sharing the same turf.

A mob of gray kangaroos on the alert.

Food Processor

Most kangaroos eat mainly grass, although they will gladly add any other green plant they come across to their menu. Often the grass they eat is not the nice soft type you find on your lawn. Some of it is quite coarse, but this is not a problem for the kangaroo. Its two lower front teeth jut forward like scissor blades for snipping off grass and small twigs.

Like cows, sheep and goats, kangaroos do not digest their food all at once. They swallow it, then later bring it back into their mouth as cud for more chewing. The food is finally digested when the kangaroo is resting. Only the musky rat kangaroo, which eats mainly insects and worms, does not need to break its food down this way.

Most kangaroos must drink water regularly and therefore like to feed near streams or waterholes.

There's nothing like a cool refreshing drink on a hot day!

Stop, Look and Listen

If you tried to sneak up on a kangaroo, you would probably be wasting your time. Kangaroos are very shy and so they are always on the alert. In fact, they never seem to relax completely, not even when they're sleeping. Mostly, they take short naps, getting up often to look, listen and sniff for danger.

Should there be anything at all threatening around, the kangaroo will likely detect it since it has very keen senses. Those big dark brown eyes can see far into the distance, and the large rounded ears can be turned in any direction to pick up even the faintest sounds, wherever they are coming from. Kangaroos also seem to have an excellent sense of smell.

"Follow me!"

Clean Living

Keeping clean is important to a kangaroo. It removes ticks and fleas with its forepaws or with the claws on its second and third toes. You may be surprised to learn that a kangaroo cleans its coat just like your pet cat does. It licks its front paws and runs them over its fur to remove dirt and smooth down the hairs. Joeys get help with their grooming from their mother. A daily bath with mom's tongue keeps them clean.

Some types of kangaroos may even take a bath in a river or lake to wash themselves. The smaller varieties are often quite good swimmers while the larger ones are more awkward in the water.

Kick Boxing

Kangaroos are usually gentle animals—until two males are interested in the same female or an "old man's" authority is challenged by another male. Then there is only one way to settle the disagreement—a boxing match!

Round one begins with a loud cough. Next the two combatants strut stiffly, sizing each other up and waiting for an opening. Standing on their hind legs, they begin to throw punches. As the battle heats up they may lean on their tails and kick with one or both feet. Each boxer must be careful to avoid its opponent's sharp claws. Sometimes one kangaroo may pick up the other and toss him through the air!

While most fighting ends without either animal coming to any harm, injuries do sometimes occur.

Overleaf:
Getting ready to throw the first punch.

Dingo Danger

Life can be dangerous for the kangaroo. The young are the most vulnerable and must always be on the lookout for pythons, large lizards and birds of prey. But the greatest danger of all to young and old alike is the dingo, Australia's wild dog.

At the first sign of danger a kangaroo may stamp its feet or give a loud warning call. Immediately other nearby kangaroos scatter in all directions. Although kangaroos would rather run away than fight, they will defend themselves if cornered, striking out with their big strong feet and sharp toenails. A kangaroo's kick can kill a dingo instantly.

If there is any hint of danger, the joey stays very close to its mother.

G'day, Mate!

Different species of kangaroos mate at different times of the year. In the case of some wallabies, for instance, the mating season is very short and most of the babies are born in late January. Gray kangaroos, on the other hand, are capable of mating anytime during the year. However, they tend to time things so that the young are born in summer and leave the pouch the following spring.

When a female kangaroo is ready to mate, a male will follow her, pawing at her tail. Males compete for the females—often the largest and strongest male will mate with the doe. In fact, in a mob, one male—often the "old man"—will father most of the offspring. Courtship may last for a few hours or up to two or three days. After that, the couple separates. The mother will give birth and raise her baby alone.

Incredible Journey

About one month after mating, the baby is born. Most species of kangaroos give birth to only one baby, although there are occasionally twins. Musky rat kangaroos are the only ones that usually give birth to twins.

Many animals go to a lot of trouble to find and prepare a safe place for their young before they are born. Not the mother kangaroo, however. She has a built-in home for her babies—on her abdomen!

Just before she gives birth the doe cleans her pouch. The newborn kangaroo, or joey, is born outside the pouch. No bigger than a jellybean, it is hairless and blind and almost totally helpless. Its front legs are well developed, however, and the joey uses them to crawl through the fur of its mother's belly, following a trail that she has licked from below her tail to the pouch. Once safely inside the warm pouch, the newborn attaches itself to one of its mother's four nipples and nurses on her milk.

Thanks to its mother's nourishing milk, this quokka joey has grown quickly. Its ears and eyes are now well developed, but for the moment it still seems quite happy to observe the world from the cozy safety of its mother's pouch.

Home Sweet Home

The inside of its mother's dark, warm pocket is the joey's home for the next few months. As time passes the youngster grows fur and develops eyes, ears, back legs and a tail. When the joey is five or more months old, it peeps out at the world for the first time. It cannot reach the ground from inside the pouch but when mom bends down to feed on the grass, the joey nibbles a bit too.

Soon it is time for the joey to try out its legs. At first it only leaves the pouch for short periods, and its mother is careful not to let her baby out of her sight.

Not all joeys are anxious to leave the security of the pouch, however. Sometimes the mother kangaroo has to encourage her young one a bit by bending down and tipping it out onto the ground.

Male and female joeys are about the same size as long as they are living in the pouch. Once they are living outside the pouch, males start growing faster. By the time they are adults, the males may be up to twice the size of females.

Opposite page:
When a joey jumps back into the pouch, it often ends up with its legs sticking out until it gets settled.

Growing Up

Gradually, the joey begins to spend more time outside the pouch—but it never strays very far. And at the first sign of danger, the young kangaroo dives headfirst back into the pouch, does a complete somersault inside, then peeks outside to see if all is clear!

Joeys are very playful and enjoy wrestling and frolicking with each other. Sometimes they have boxing matches, but these are all in good fun.

As the joey grows the pouch expands, but after about 8 to 10 months the young kangaroo has outgrown its mobile home. It will continue to need its mother's care for some time yet, but even if it wants to return to the pouch she will not let it back in.

At one and a half to two years old, a female kangaroo is ready to start a family of her own. Usually she stays in the mob where she was born, but a young male normally leaves to take up his life as a boomer—and perhaps someday as the "old man" in a new mob.

Words to Know

Blue Flier   A female red kangaroo which is a blue-gray color and can travel quickly.

Boomer   A male kangaroo.

Doe   A female kangaroo.

Joey   A baby kangaroo.

Macropod   From *Macropodidae*, the scientific name for the kangaroo family. Literally, "big foot."

Marsupials   A class of mammals whose females carry their young in a pouch until they are fully developed.

Mate   To come together to produce young. Either member of an animal pair is also the other's mate.

Mob   A herd of kangaroos.

Nipple   The part of the mother's body through which a baby drinks her milk.

"Old Man"   Leader of a kangaroo mob.

Pouch   The fur-lined pocket of the female marsupial where the baby lives until it is fully developed.

Quokka   A kind of wallaby found only in a few places in southwestern Australia.

Tendon   A tough, strong band or cord of tissue that attaches a muscle to a bone (or to some other part).

INDEX

Cover Photo: Jim Grace (Photo Researchers)

Photo Credits: Heidi Ecker (Focus Stock Photo), page 4; Breck P. Kent, pages 7, 11, 15, 31; John Cancalosi, pages 8, 12-13, 19, 22, 43; Bill Ivy, page 16; Eugen Schuhmacher (WWF-Photolibrary), page 21; Michael Simmons (Focus Stock Photo), page 24; Tom McHugh (Photo Researchers), page 27; Dr. E.R. Degginger, page 28; Len Lee Rue III, pages 32, 36-37; Len Rue Jr., page 40; Dallas Heaton (Canapress/Uniphoto Picture Agency), page 39; Kraseman (Peter Arnold/ Hot Shots), page 45.